IN THE WORD:

Walking through the Book of James

A 21-Day Personal Study

Allison Myers

WESTBOW
PRESS®
A DIVISION OF THOMAS NELSON
& ZONDERVAN

WestBow Press books may be ordered through booksellers or by contacting:

WestBow Press
A Division of Thomas Nelson & Zondervan
1663 Liberty Drive
Bloomington, IN 47403
www.westbowpress.com
844-714-3454

Scripture quotations are from the ESV® Bible (The Holy Bible, English Standard Version®), Copyright © 2001 by Crossway, a publishing ministry of Good News Publishers. Used by permission. All rights reserved.

ISBN: 978-1-6642-4503-7 (sc)
ISBN: 978-1-6642-4502-0 (e)

Print information available on the last page.

WestBow Press rev. date: 10/13/2021

INTRODUCTION

When I first became a Christian at the age of twenty-six, I literally knew almost NOTHING about the Bible, let alone about theology, church history, apologetics, and the list goes on and on. So, I spent those first few years of my newfound salvation ravenously reading as much as I could related to Christianity, obviously including the Bible plus many other works by Christian authors. Along the way, I discovered that the words of Jesus amazed me, I loved the writings of C. S. Lewis, my cherished *Lord of the Rings* was actually a Christian allegory, America had been the home of a powerful Christian intellectual by the name of Jonathan Edwards.... In other words, it was a complete nerdfest, and I loved it.

As the years went by, I was blessed to become married and have three delightful children, which, albeit wonderful, also put a cramp in my reading and Bible study to say the least. Instead of poring over Paul's letters, I was becoming well versed in *Peppa Pig*, all while learning how to quickly build Legos and trying to stop the seemingly endless amount of toys from taking over our home. And one day, I realized that I just wasn't that great at reading the Bible any longer. It wasn't that I didn't love Jesus or love His Word; it was that life had become a bit chaotic, and it seemed easier to neglect the Bible than a sobbing, screaming, or potentially poopy child. Sure, I still completed small group Bible studies and read devotionals here and there, but was I personally slowing down to ingest the Bible for myself? Was I really studying God's Word on my own and listening to what He had to say to me? Not really.

What struck me is that if I was having such a hard time really working through the Scriptures, then I couldn't be alone, right? I couldn't be the *only* one who felt as though I wasn't taking the time to study God's Word personally. Thus came the idea for this devotional. My goal and hope is to give people who are struggling to read God's Word consistently *for themselves* a chance to take a book of the Bible in bite-sized pieces and, day by day, work their way through the Scripture, reflect on what it says, and pray through it. While God's Word is so precious, I also understand that sometimes the reality of treating it as well as it deserves can be a bit of a challenge. I'm praying that this tool will enable us to honor the Bible by taking it slowly and hearing what God has to tell us, as we walk (not run or rush) through His Word.

Things to Note:

1. Begin Each Day with a Prayer
    Every time we open the Scriptures, it's helpful to say a quick prayer, asking God to speak to us through His Word. So, before you begin to read through each day, take a moment to pray that God would help you to understand His precious Word.

2. The Amount of Scripture Per Day
    As stated above, I tried to break up a chosen book of the Bible into bite-sized pieces to enable its reader not to feel overwhelmed by the amount of reading. Some days have more verses, and some days have less, depending on the complexity of the text.

3. Questions for Reflection
    Each day the reader has three questions to reflect upon what has just been read. This enables the reader to take a deeper look at the day's Scripture and make sure he or she really understands what God's Word is saying.

4. Application

   Each day also provides readers the opportunity to write down a verse from the day's Scripture that spoke to them the most. There's something powerful about writing something down (let alone God's Word). In fact, a 2014 study showed that note taking with an actual pen or pencil helps you to learn information effectively. One reason is because "parts of the brain associated with learning work far better and more actively when someone is asked to reproduce something in a freehand, written way, as opposed to tracing or typing out what was shown."[1] Here's hoping the Word of God becomes engrained in our hearts, souls, and minds.

5. End by Praying through God's Word

   Each day ends with a prayer that takes the reader through what the day's Scripture was about. The goal is to pray God's Word over our lives because we believe in its authority, truth, and ability to change us. May the Lord transform us to look more and more like His Son Jesus.

6. How Long Should Each Day Take?

   Each day should take the reader about 10-15 minutes to read, respond, and pray.

In the end, the Word of God is living, active, and sharper than any two-edged sword. May we be the kind of people who take God's Word seriously, read it, contemplate it, pray it over our lives, and, by the grace of God, live it. I pray that this book is a blessing to you and that the Word of God will wash over you, change you, and conform you more to the magnificent image of Christ Jesus.

QUICK FACTS ON THE BOOK OF JAMES

Author: James, the brother of Jesus and a leader in the Jerusalem church

When Written: Likely in the mid-40s

Written To (but applicable to all Christians): The 12 tribes in the Dispersion, which are Jewish Christians living outside of Palestine

DAY 1

JAMES 1:1-8

1 James, a servant of God and of the Lord Jesus Christ, To the twelve tribes in the Dispersion: Greetings. ²Count it all joy, my brothers, when you meet trials of various kinds, ³for you know that the testing of your faith produces steadfastness. ⁴And let steadfastness have its full effect, that you may be perfect and complete, lacking in nothing.

⁵If any of you lacks wisdom, let him ask God, who gives generously to all without reproach, and it will be given him. ⁶But let him ask in faith, with no doubting, for the one who doubts is like a wave of the sea that is driven and tossed by the wind. ⁷For that person must not suppose that he will receive anything from the Lord; ⁸he is a double-minded man, unstable in all his ways.

Reflecting on God's Word:

1. James calls us to respond to life's trials with joy, knowing that God is using them to grow us (v. 2-4). Note that James says WHEN you meet trials—the expectation is that believers will, indeed, suffer here on earth. Why are believers often surprised by suffering? What are we forgetting when we are surprised by life's pain?

_____

_____

_____

_____

2. When have you experienced a trial that produced steadfastness (being resolute or unwavering) in your faith? How did that experience change you?

_____

_____

_____

_____

_____

3. According to verse 5, where does wisdom come from? How is this different from the world's view of wisdom?

_____

_____

_____

_____

_____

Application:

Rewrite (either verbatim or in your own words) the verse from today's Scripture that spoke to you the most. How will you apply today's Scripture in your life?

_____

_____

_____

_____

_____

Praying Through God's Word:

Father God, help me to respond to life's trials with joy knowing that You are working in and through them. Lord, give me wisdom as I walk on this earth and give me great faith to trust You all the days of my life. In Jesus' name I pray. Amen.

DAY 2

JAMES 1:9-15

⁹ Let the lowly brother boast in his exaltation, ¹⁰ and the rich in his humiliation, because like a flower of the grass he will pass away. ¹¹ For the sun rises with its scorching heat and withers the grass; its flower falls, and its beauty perishes. So also will the rich man fade away in the midst of his pursuits.

¹² Blessed is the man who remains steadfast under trial, for when he has stood the test he will receive the crown of life, which God has promised to those who love him. ¹³ Let no one say when he is tempted, "I am being tempted by God," for God cannot be tempted with evil, and he himself tempts no one. ¹⁴ But each person is tempted when he is lured and enticed by his own desire. ¹⁵ Then desire when it has conceived gives birth to sin, and sin when it is fully grown brings forth death.

Reflecting on God's Word:

1. According to verses 9-11, will the wealthy be saved from death by their riches? How does this help us understand why God must be our ultimate treasure?

_____

_____

_____

_____

_____

2. In verse 12 we again see the idea of trials revealing whether we are steadfast in our faith. We also see a link between steadfast faith and loving God. How do our trials reveal whether or not we truly love God?

_____

_____

_____

_____

_____

3. According to verse 14, what leads people into temptation? Why do we often blame others and/or God for our personal sins?

_____

_____

_____

_____

_____

Application:

Rewrite (either verbatim or in your own words) the verse from today's Scripture that spoke to you the most. How will you apply today's Scripture in your life?

_____

_____

_____

_____

_____

Praying Through God's Word:

Father God, thank You that You do not judge us by how successful we are in the world's eyes, but that You love and value all people. Help me to love You with all of my heart, soul, strength, and mind. Thank You for Your Son, Jesus, who took the punishment for my sin, Lord. It's in His precious name that I pray. Amen.

DAY 3

JAMES 1:16-21

[16] Do not be deceived, my beloved brothers. [17] Every good gift and every perfect gift is from above, coming down from the Father of lights, with whom there is no variation or shadow due to change. [18] Of his own will he brought us forth by the word of truth, that we should be a kind of firstfruits of his creatures.

[19] Know this, my beloved brothers: let every person be quick to hear, slow to speak, slow to anger; [20] for the anger of man does not produce the righteousness of God. [21] Therefore put away all filthiness and rampant wickedness and receive with meekness the implanted word, which is able to save your souls.

Reflecting on God's Word:

1. Today's verses reveal that God does not vary or change (v. 17). What are some things that have changed dramatically in your life? Why do you think God wants us to know He is unchangeable?

_____

_____

_____

_____

_____

2. Verse 19 tells us that we should be quick to hear, slow to speak, and slow to anger. Which of the three is the most challenging for you? Why?

_____

_____

_____

_____

_____

3. Much has been written about the phrase "implanted word" in verse 21. For some, the phrase means that the Word of God is actually rooted in your heart. What do you think it means for God's Word to be rooted in your heart? How is this different from just knowing what the Bible says?

_____

_____

_____

_____

_____

Application:

Rewrite (either verbatim or in your own words) the verse from today's Scriptures that spoke to you the most. How will you apply today's Scripture in your life?

_____

_____

_____

_____

_____

Praying Through God's Word:

Father God, thank You for all of the things You have done for me. Help me to be grateful for all that You have provided. Help me to be quick to hear, slow to speak, and slow to anger, Lord. Please let Your word be deeply rooted in my heart. I ask for all of this in Jesus' precious name. Amen.

DAY 4

JAMES 1:22-27

²² But be doers of the word, and not hearers only, deceiving yourselves. ²³ For if anyone is a hearer of the word and not a doer, he is like a man who looks intently at his natural face in a mirror. ²⁴ For he looks at himself and goes away and at once forgets what he was like. ²⁵ But the one who looks into the perfect law, the law of liberty, and perseveres, being no hearer who forgets but a doer who acts, he will be blessed in his doing.

²⁶ If anyone thinks he is religious and does not bridle his tongue but deceives his heart, this person's religion is worthless. ²⁷ Religion that is pure and undefiled before God the Father is this: to visit orphans and widows in their affliction, and to keep oneself unstained from the world.

Reflecting on God's Word:

1. Verse 22 says that if we only hear the Word of God but don't act on it, then we deceive ourselves. Why do we deceive (to fool or delude) ourselves when we hear but don't act?

_____

_____

_____

_____

2. What does verse 26 say an unbridled (uncontrolled, unrestrained) tongue reveals about our religion? What do our words reveal about the state of our hearts?

_____

_____

_____

_____

_____

3. What do you think it means to be "unstained" from the world (v. 27)? How do we live in the world and remain unstained?

_____

_____

_____

_____

_____

Application:

Rewrite (either verbatim or in your own words) the verse from today's Scriptures that spoke to you the most. How will you apply today's Scripture in your life?

_____

_____

_____

_____

_____

Praying Through God's Word:

Dear Father, help me to be a doer of Your Word. Help me to bridle my tongue and speak in ways that are pleasing to You and honor You, Lord. Help me to care for those who are afflicted in this world and enable me to see opportunities to help them. Keep me unstained from the world, and also help me to understand how I should live among those who don't know You. In Jesus' name I pray. Amen.

DAY 5

JAMES 2:1-7

My brothers, show no partiality as you hold the faith in our Lord Jesus Christ, the Lord of glory. ² For if a man wearing a gold ring and fine clothing comes into your assembly, and a poor man in shabby clothing also comes in, ³ and if you pay attention to the one who wears the fine clothing and say, "You sit here in a good place," while you say to the poor man, "You stand over there," or, "Sit down at my feet," ⁴ have you not then made distinctions among yourselves and become judges with evil thoughts?

⁵ Listen, my beloved brothers, has not God chosen those who are poor in the world to be rich in faith and heirs of the kingdom, which he has promised to those who love him? ⁶ But you have dishonored the poor man. Are not the rich the ones who oppress you, and the ones who drag you into court? ⁷ Are they not the ones who blaspheme the honorable name by which you were called?

Reflecting on God's Word:

1. According to verse 4, when we show favoritism, we make distinctions and judge others with evil thoughts. Upon what sorts of things do humans tend to judge one another? How is this different from how God judges?

_____

_____

_____

_____

_____

2. What do you learn about the heart of God in verse 5? How is His attitude towards the poor different from ours?

_____

_____

_____

_____

_____

3. Why do you think humans tend to honor the rich? What does it reveal about our hearts?

_____

_____

_____

_____

_____

Application:

Rewrite (either verbatim or in your own words) the verse from today's Scriptures that spoke to you the most. How will you apply today's Scripture in your life?

_____

_____

_____

_____

_____

Praying Through God's Word:

Dear Lord, help me to see the world as You do. Help me to not show favoritism to any. Help me to love people as You do and understand that their worth comes from You and not from what they have or don't have. Help me to care about the rich and poor alike, as I seek to share Your Gospel with all whom I encounter. In Jesus' name I pray. Amen.

DAY 6

JAMES 2:8-13

[8] If you really fulfill the royal law according to the Scripture, "You shall love your neighbor as yourself," you are doing well. [9] But if you show partiality, you are committing sin and are convicted by the law as transgressors. [10] For whoever keeps the whole law but fails in one point has become guilty of all of it. [11] For he who said, "Do not commit adultery," also said, "Do not murder." If you do not commit adultery but do murder, you have become a transgressor of the law. [12] So speak and so act as those who are to be judged under the law of liberty. [13] For judgment is without mercy to one who has shown no mercy. Mercy triumphs over judgment.

Reflecting on God's Word:

1. What is God's royal law in verse 8? Why do you think this is so important to Him?

_____

_____

_____

_____

_____

2. According to verses 10-11, breaking one of God's laws results in breaking His entire law because the punishment for sin, in general, is

the same. Based on these verses, how would you respond to people who think their good works will outweigh their bad ones?

_____

_____

_____

_____

_____

3. Verse 13 speaks of mercy (having compassion or showing forgiveness towards someone whom you have the power to punish). How is God merciful to us? Why do you think He expects us to be merciful to others?

_____

_____

_____

_____

_____

Application:

Rewrite (either verbatim or in your own words) the verse from today's Scriptures that spoke to you the most. How will you apply today's Scripture in your life?

_____

_____

_____

_____

_____

Praying Through God's Word:

Dear Father, help me to be the kind of person who loves my neighbor as myself. God, help me to live a life that is pleasing to You and is in obedience to Your perfect Law. Give me the grace to be merciful to others and understand how merciful You have been towards me. In Jesus' name I pray. Amen.

DAY 7

JAMES 2:14-19

[14] What good is it, my brothers, if someone says he has faith but does not have works? Can that faith save him? [15] If a brother or sister is poorly clothed and lacking in daily food, [16] and one of you says to them, "Go in peace, be warmed and filled," without giving them the things needed for the body, what good is that? [17] So also faith by itself, if it does not have works, is dead. [18] But someone will say, "You have faith and I have works." Show me your faith apart from your works, and I will show you my faith by my works. [19] You believe that God is one; you do well. Even the demons believe—and shudder!

Reflecting on God's Word:

1. In today's verses, James stresses that true, saving faith will be accompanied by works. Why is faith not saving without works? Why are works not saving without faith?

_____

_____

_____

_____

2. What do you think it means in verse 17 that faith without works is dead? Who is someone you know whose faith seems "alive"? What makes their faith seem alive?

_____

_____

_____

_____

_____

3. According to verse 19, why is it not enough to just believe in God? What do you think is the difference between what demons and what Christians believe about God? How do these different beliefs result in different actions?

_____

_____

_____

_____

_____

Application:

Rewrite (either verbatim or in your own words) the verse from today's Scriptures that spoke to you the most. How will you apply today's Scripture in your life?

_____

_____

_____

_____

_____

Praying Through God's Word:

Dear Lord, I pray that I would be the kind of person who lives out my faith and shows the world Your love and Your goodness. Help me to remember that my works don't save me but are merely an outward expression of believing in You and the change that You bring to those who know You. In Jesus' name I pray. Amen.

DAY 8

JAMES 2:20-26

20 Do you want to be shown, you foolish person, that faith apart from works is useless? 21 Was not Abraham our father justified by works when he offered up his son Isaac on the altar? 22 You see that faith was active along with his works, and faith was completed by his works; 23 and the Scripture was fulfilled that says, "Abraham believed God, and it was counted to him as righteousness"—and he was called a friend of God. 24 You see that a person is justified by works and not by faith alone. 25 And in the same way was not also Rahab the prostitute justified by works when she received the messengers and sent them out by another way? 26 For as the body apart from the spirit is dead, so also faith apart from works is dead.

Reflecting on God's Word:

1. Today's verses again show, using two examples (Abraham and Rahab), that true faith reveals itself through works. How would you respond to someone who claimed his works alone justified him before God? Is that biblical according to today's verses (see verse 22)?

_____

_____

_____

_____

2. Verse 23 tells us Abraham was called a friend of God. What do you think it means to be God's friend? What does that reveal about God Himself?

_____

_____

_____

_____

_____

3. According to verse 25, what was Rahab previously known for? Why do you think James chose to have Rahab be an example of faith revealing itself through works? What do you think he wants us to learn?

_____

_____

_____

_____

_____

Application:

Rewrite (either verbatim or in your own words) the verse from today's Scriptures that spoke to you the most. How will you apply today's Scripture in your life?

_____

_____

_____

_____

_____

Praying Through God's Word:

Dear Father, grant me saving faith that changes my actions, my speech, and my thoughts. Help me to live a life that is pleasing to You. I pray that I would also be considered a friend of God. Please help me to know You more and more, Lord. Thank You that despite our pasts, You are willing to forgive us of our sins and change us, God. In Jesus' name I pray. Amen.

DAY 9

JAMES 3:1-5

3 Not many of you should become teachers, my brothers, for you know that we who teach will be judged with greater strictness. ² For we all stumble in many ways. And if anyone does not stumble in what he says, he is a perfect man, able also to bridle his whole body. ³ If we put bits into the mouths of horses so that they obey us, we guide their whole bodies as well. ⁴ Look at the ships also: though they are so large and are driven by strong winds, they are guided by a very small rudder wherever the will of the pilot directs. ⁵ So also the tongue is a small member, yet it boasts of great things. How great a forest is set ablaze by such a small fire!

Reflecting on God's Word:

1. Verse 2 says if you can speak without error, then you are the kind of person who can control your entire body perfectly as well. In other words, to be able to tame the tongue is to be able to tame all. Why do you think it's so difficult for people to tame their tongues/their speech?

_____

_____

_____

_____

2. In light of verse 2, why do you think Paul cautions in verse 1 against many people wanting to be teachers?

_____

_____

_____

_____

_____

3. Verses 3-5 describe something very small controlling something way beyond its size. What do we learn about the power of the tongue? Why should we be careful with our words?

_____

_____

_____

_____

_____

Application:

Rewrite (either verbatim or in your own words) the verse from today's Scriptures that spoke to you the most. How will you apply today's Scripture in your life?

_____

_____

_____

_____

_____

Praying Through God's Word:

Dear Father God, help us to tame our tongues. Help us to be mindful of our words. Help us to understand the power of the tongue. Give us godly speech, and help us to speak Your Truth in love, Lord. In Jesus' name I pray. Amen.

DAY 10

JAMES 3:6-8

⁶ And the tongue is a fire, a world of unrighteousness. The tongue is set among our members, staining the whole body, setting on fire the entire course of life, and set on fire by hell. ⁷ For every kind of beast and bird, of reptile and sea creature, can be tamed and has been tamed by mankind, ⁸ but no human being can tame the tongue. It is a restless evil, full of deadly poison.

Reflecting on God's Word:

1. In today's verses, James uses the idea of fire repeatedly. What does fire have the potential to do? Why do you think James uses this word again and again to describe the tongue?

_____
_____
_____
_____
_____

2. What does it mean in verse 6 that the tongue stains our entire body? Also, what do you think it means that the tongue sets "on fire the entire course of life"?

_____
_____
_____
_____

3. According to verse 7, what CAN humans tame? What does verse 8 tell us NO human can tame? What does this reveal about the human heart and our need for a Savior?

_____

_____

_____

_____

_____

Application:

Rewrite (either verbatim or in your own words) the verse from today's Scriptures that spoke to you the most. How will you apply today's Scripture in your life?

_____

_____

_____

_____

_____

Praying Through God's Word:

Dear Lord, help us to understand the weighty nature of our tongues. Help us to understand that we are incapable of speaking well apart from You, God. I pray that the Holy Spirit would help me in my speech, in my words, and in my heart. In Jesus' name I pray. Amen.

DAY 11

JAMES 3:9-12

⁹ With it we bless our Lord and Father, and with it we curse people who are made in the likeness of God. ¹⁰ From the same mouth come blessing and cursing. My brothers, these things ought not to be so. ¹¹ Does a spring pour forth from the same opening both fresh and salt water? ¹² Can a fig tree, my brothers, bear olives, or a grapevine produce figs? Neither can a salt pond yield fresh water.

Reflecting on God's Word:

1. Here we see the contradictory nature of the tongue—capable of saying both wonderful and wicked things. For the believer, "these things ought not to be so" (v. 10). Why is it so important for Christians to be careful with their words? Based on what we've learned about the tongue thus far, why will this be a challenge?

_____

_____

_____

_____

_____

2. James reveals we not only curse people, but that we do so to those _made in the likeness of God_ (v. 9). Why is it important to remember that God has made ALL of us and has given His likeness to ALL? How should that help us with our speech?

_____

_____

_____

_____

_____

3. A grapevine's being unable to produce figs is a reminder that believers should be aware of the fruit we are producing. What kind of "verbal fruit" seems incompatible with the life of a Christian?

_____

_____

_____

_____

_____

Application:

Rewrite (either verbatim or in your own words) the verse from today's Scriptures that spoke to you the most. How will you apply today's Scripture in your life?

_____

_____

_____

_____

_____

Praying Through God's Word:

Dear Father God, I pray that You would help me speak in ways that are pleasing to You. Help me not to have a tongue that is full of contradiction. I pray that my tongue would bear fruit that is in line with the life of someone who knows You and is filled with Your Spirit. Help me to see others as bearing Your likeness and loved by You. I ask for all of these things in Jesus' name. Amen.

DAY 12

JAMES 3:13-18

13 Who is wise and understanding among you? By his good conduct let him show his works in the meekness of wisdom. 14 But if you have bitter jealousy and selfish ambition in your hearts, do not boast and be false to the truth. 15 This is not the wisdom that comes down from above, but is earthly, unspiritual, demonic. 16 For where jealousy and selfish ambition exist, there will be disorder and every vile practice. 17 But the wisdom from above is first pure, then peaceable, gentle, open to reason, full of mercy and good fruits, impartial and sincere. 18 And a harvest of righteousness is sown in peace by those who make peace.

Reflecting on God's Word:

1. As verse 13 tells us, godly wisdom results in actions that are done in meekness (humility, gentleness). Why should wisdom that is given to us from God naturally produce humility?

_____

_____

_____

_____

2. James shows the difference between the wisdom of God and the wisdom of the world. According to these verses, what kinds of actions accompany worldly wisdom? (see verses 14-16)

_____

_____

_____

_____

_____

3. Godly wisdom is known for being peaceable (v. 17-18). Why do you think these two things—godly wisdom and loving peace—go hand in hand?

_____

_____

_____

_____

_____

Application:

Rewrite (either verbatim or in your own words) the verse from today's Scriptures that spoke to you the most. How will you apply today's Scripture in your life?

_____

_____

_____

_____

_____

Praying Through God's Word:

Dear God, I pray that You would give me Your wisdom, Lord. Help me to be the kind of person who acts in humility and with meekness. I pray that I would cast off the wisdom of the world and see it for what it truly is: foolishness. Give me the grace to be the kind of person who makes peace whenever it is possible. I ask for these things in Jesus' name. Amen.

DAY 13

JAMES 4:1-6

4 What causes quarrels and what causes fights among you? Is it not this, that your passions are at war within you? **2** You desire and do not have, so you murder. You covet and cannot obtain, so you fight and quarrel. You do not have, because you do not ask. **3** You ask and do not receive, because you ask wrongly, to spend it on your passions. **4** You adulterous people! Do you not know that friendship with the world is enmity with God? Therefore whoever wishes to be a friend of the world makes himself an enemy of God. **5** Or do you suppose it is to no purpose that the Scripture says, "He yearns jealously over the spirit that he has made to dwell in us"? **6** But he gives more grace. Therefore it says, "God opposes the proud but gives grace to the humble."

Reflecting on God's Word:

1. According to verse 1, what causes fights among people? How should that help us understand why God at times says no to some of our prayers (see verse 3)?

---

2. What do you think it means to be a friend of the world (v. 4)? If you love the world, then why would that automatically make you an enemy of God? Why are the two incompatible?

_____

_____

_____

_____

_____

3. God has given believers His Holy Spirit and even more grace on top of that (verses 5-6). Why, then, do you think we're considered adulterers when we love the world more than we love God?

_____

_____

_____

_____

_____

Application:

Rewrite (either verbatim or in your own words) the verse from today's Scriptures that spoke to you the most. How will you apply today's Scripture in your life?

_____

_____

_____

_____

_____

Praying Through God's Word:

Dear God, thank You for Your many kindnesses and Your immeasurable grace in my life. Help me to not love the world or the things of this world, Lord, but to put You first in my heart and in my life. In Jesus' name I pray. Amen.

DAY 14

JAMES 4:7-10

7 Submit yourselves therefore to God. Resist the devil, and he will flee from you. 8 Draw near to God, and he will draw near to you. Cleanse your hands, you sinners, and purify your hearts, you double-minded. 9 Be wretched and mourn and weep. Let your laughter be turned to mourning and your joy to gloom. 10 Humble yourselves before the Lord, and he will exalt you.

Reflecting on God's Word:

1. What do you think it means to submit yourself to God (v. 7)? What would a life submitted to God look like on a day-to-day basis?

_____

_____

_____

_____

_____

2. As humans, our tendency is to be double-minded (divided in interest), sinful, and possessing of an unclean heart, which is why James says we are to weep when we recognize the truth about what we really are (v. 9-10). What is the world's opinion of mankind? How does it differ dramatically from what the Scriptures teach?

_____

_____

_____

_____

3. While the world tells us to exalt ourselves, the Bible says we should humble ourselves. According to today's verses, WHO should exalt us? (see verse 10) Why is self-exaltation sinful?

_____

_____

_____

_____

_____

Application:

Rewrite (either verbatim or in your own words) the verse from today's Scriptures that spoke to you the most. How will you apply today's Scripture in your life?

_____

_____

_____

_____

_____

Praying Through God's Word:

Dear God, help me to live a life that easily and readily submits to You. Enable me to resist the evil one and draw close to You, Lord. Help me to understand the truth about human nature and to live a life of humility. I ask for these things in Jesus' name. Amen.

DAY 15

JAMES 4:11-12

[11] Do not speak evil against one another, brothers. The one who speaks against a brother or judges his brother, speaks evil against the law and judges the law. But if you judge the law, you are not a doer of the law but a judge. [12] There is only one lawgiver and judge, he who is able to save and to destroy. But who are you to judge your neighbor?

Reflecting on God's Word:

1. Verse 11's "speak evil" translates the ancient Greek word *katalalia*, which is "the sin of those who meet in corners and gather in little groups and pass on confidential information which destroy the good name of those who are not there to defend themselves."[2] What makes this kind of speech evil? Why is this kind of talk inappropriate for the people of God?

_____

_____

_____

_____

_____

2. We become judges of God's law (v. 11) when we judge other Christians. This is because God's law was meant to reveal our sin, so when we judge others, "we put ourselves in the same place as the

law, in effect judging the law."[3] Knowing what God's word says about humanity, why are we not fit to judge God's law?

_____

_____

_____

_____

_____

3. Who is the only lawgiver and judge (v. 12)? Why is He fit to judge? Why are in incapable of judging (or condemning) our neighbor?

_____

_____

_____

_____

_____

Application:

Rewrite (either verbatim or in your own words) the verse from today's Scriptures that spoke to you the most. How will you apply today's Scripture in your life?

_____

_____

_____

_____

_____

Praying Through God's Word:

Dear God, help me not to speak evil of others. Lord, enable me to see that there is only One, True Judge, and it is not me. Grant me the humility to understand that I have no right to stand as judge before my fellow man. In Jesus' name I pray. Amen.

DAY 16

JAMES 4:13-17

¹³ Come now, you who say, "Today or tomorrow we will go into such and such a town and spend a year there and trade and make a profit"—¹⁴ yet you do not know what tomorrow will bring. What is your life? For you are a mist that appears for a little time and then vanishes. ¹⁵ Instead you ought to say, "If the Lord wills, we will live and do this or that." ¹⁶ As it is, you boast in your arrogance. All such boasting is evil. ¹⁷ So whoever knows the right thing to do and fails to do it, for him it is sin.

Reflecting on God's Word:

1. According to verses 13-14, why shouldn't we speak about our future plans with certainty?

_____

_____

_____

_____

2. Verse 15 gives us another reason why we ought to be humble—our lives are in the hands of God. If we understand that God is ultimately in control, how should that bring us comfort and peace here on earth?

_____

_____

_____

_____

3. A new, expanded definition of sin is given to us in verse 17. How does this verse define sin? How does this definition of sin differ from the world's view of it?

_____

_____

_____

_____

_____

Application:

Rewrite (either verbatim or in your own words) the verse from today's Scriptures that spoke to you the most. How will you apply today's Scripture in your life?

_____

_____

_____

_____

_____

Praying Through God's Word:

Dear Father God, give me the grace to understand that my life is completely in Your hands and that I am not in control. Lord, help me to do what is right and not be lazy or complacent about doing what I know to be right. God, help me to understand the depths of my sin and my desperate need of Your forgiveness, which comes through Your Son Jesus alone. It's in His precious name that I pray. Amen.

DAY 17

JAMES 5:1-6

5 Come now, you rich, weep and howl for the miseries that are coming upon you. ² Your riches have rotted and your garments are moth-eaten. ³ Your gold and silver have corroded, and their corrosion will be evidence against you and will eat your flesh like fire. You have laid up treasure in the last days. ⁴ Behold, the wages of the laborers who mowed your fields, which you kept back by fraud, are crying out against you, and the cries of the harvesters have reached the ears of the Lord of hosts. ⁵ You have lived on the earth in luxury and in self-indulgence. You have fattened your hearts in a day of slaughter. ⁶ You have condemned and murdered the righteous person. He does not resist you.

Reflecting on God's Word:

1. Again in the Book of James, we see its author speak of the destruction that will come upon the rich unbelievers. In verses 1-3, how does James describe what will happen to their treasures? What are the only things in life that are eternal? How does that help us to understand the Scripture's condemnation of storing up earthly treasures?

_____

_____

_____

_____

2. According to verses 4-6, what are some of the crimes of these rich individuals?

_____

_____

_____

_____

_____

3. As we read earlier in James, people are made in the likeness of God. Why then would the mistreatment of others, particularly for the gain of money, greatly anger the Lord?

_____

_____

_____

_____

_____

Application:

Rewrite (either verbatim or in your own words) the verse from today's Scriptures that spoke to you the most. How will you apply today's Scripture in your life?

_____

_____

_____

_____

_____

Praying Through God's Word:

Dear Lord, help me to understand the difference between earthly and eternal treasures. Help me to handle all that You have given me in a way that honors You and help me to take my greatest pleasure in You alone. In Jesus' name I pray. Amen.

DAY 18

JAMES 5:7-9

⁷ Be patient, therefore, brothers, until the coming of the Lord. See how the farmer waits for the precious fruit of the earth, being patient about it, until it receives the early and the late rains. ⁸ You also, be patient. Establish your hearts, for the coming of the Lord is at hand. ⁹ Do not grumble against one another, brothers, so that you may not be judged; behold, the Judge is standing at the door.

Reflecting on God's Word:

1. James tells believers to be patient as we await the return of Jesus who will one day wash away all of the sin, pain, injustice, and sickness from our world (v. 7-8). What are you personally excited about for Jesus to wash away and remedy? Why is it often hard to wait upon the Lord's justice?

_____

_____

_____

_____

_____

2. Again we see the idea of not speaking ill of (grumbling/complaining about) our sisters and brothers in Christ (v. 9). Often times, hardship makes complainers of us. What has been written in today's verses that can help us deal with our hardships in a God-honoring way?

_____

_____

_____

_____

_____

3. There's an urgency in these verses—the coming of the Lord is at hand (v. 8); the Judge is standing at the door (v. 9). In other words, Jesus could return at any moment. How well prepared do you feel for Christ's return? Does His return make you excited? Nervous? Frightened?

_____

_____

_____

_____

_____

Application:

Rewrite (either verbatim or in your own words) the verse from today's Scriptures that spoke to you the most. How will you apply today's Scripture in your life?

_____

_____

_____

_____

_____

Praying Through God's Word:

Dear God, thank You that one day You will return to remedy all that is wrong with our world. I am grateful that You have not left us here in our fallen world filled with fallen beings without any hope. Our great hope is what is to come, and for that, I am eternally grateful. Help me to be patient for Your return. Help me to be prepared for Your return. Give me the grace to lead a life that is pleasing to You. In Jesus' name I pray. Amen.

DAY 19

JAMES 5:10-12

[10] As an example of suffering and patience, brothers, take the prophets who spoke in the name of the Lord. [11] Behold, we consider those blessed who remained steadfast. You have heard of the steadfastness of Job, and you have seen the purpose of the Lord, how the Lord is compassionate and merciful. [12] But above all, my brothers, do not swear, either by heaven or by earth or by any other oath, but let your "yes" be yes and your "no" be no, so that you may not fall under condemnation.

Reflecting on God's Word:

1. James continues with the theme of having patience especially while suffering. According the verses 10-11, what other Christians does James name as examples of patient suffering? Whom personally do you know who has remained steadfast (patient/possessing endurance) amidst much suffering?

_____

_____

_____

_____

_____

2. Perhaps to our surprise, verse 11 says that suffering has a purpose and shows how the Lord is compassionate and merciful. How is the Lord compassionate and merciful in our suffering? How have you seen this personally?

_____

_____

_____

_____

_____

3. Verse 12, written in anticipation of Christ's return, again demonstrates that our words matter to God. Our "yes" should mean yes, and our "no" should mean no. Having to swear by something just reveals that our words (i.e. our character) cannot be trusted. Who is someone you know whose words you can trust? Who is someone whose words you can't trust? Why does it matter for Christians to be seen as trustworthy by others?

_____

_____

_____

_____

_____

Application:

Rewrite (either verbatim or in your own words) the verse from today's Scriptures that spoke to you the most. How will you apply today's Scripture in your life?

_____

_____

_____

_____

_____

Praying Through God's Word:

Dear Father, help me to be patient in my affliction here on earth. Give me the grace to see Your compassion and mercy towards me even in my hardships, Lord. I pray that I would be the kind of person whose word would be trustworthy. Please help me with my words, God. In Jesus' name I pray. Amen.

DAY 20

JAMES 5:13-16

¹³ Is anyone among you suffering? Let him pray. Is anyone cheerful? Let him sing praise. ¹⁴ Is anyone among you sick? Let him call for the elders of the church, and let them pray over him, anointing him with oil in the name of the Lord. ¹⁵ And the prayer of faith will save the one who is sick, and the Lord will raise him up. And if he has committed sins, he will be forgiven. ¹⁶ Therefore, confess your sins to one another and pray for one another, that you may be healed. The prayer of a righteous person has great power as it is working.

Reflecting on God's Word:

1. No matter whether you are experiencing hardship or joy, we always have a place to turn—to God (v.13-14). How quickly do you turn to God when things have gone badly? Do you turn to Him when things are going well?

_____

_____

_____

_____

_____

2. James's words convey that our prayers have great power. According to verses 14-15, what is prayer able to do?

_____

_____

_____

_____

_____

3. We know that sometimes God says no to our prayers, despite the faith that undergirds those prayers (think of Jesus in the Garden of Gethsemane). If the answer to our prayers is "no," and we are not "raised up" and "healed" here on earth (v. 15-16), how will our faith one day bring about that healing and raising up?

_____

_____

_____

_____

_____

Application:

Rewrite (either verbatim or in your own words) the verse from today's Scriptures that spoke to you the most. How will you apply today's Scripture in your life?

_____

_____

_____

_____

_____

Praying Through God's Word:

Dear God, I pray that You would help me be quick to seek You and turn to You in prayer. Lord, help me to understand that the prayers of Your people are powerful and that You hear them. God, when I don't receive an answer to prayer that I desire, help me to be patient and know that one day, we will live in a world with You where all injustice, pain, sickness, suffering, and tears have been wiped away. In Jesus' name I pray. Amen.

DAY 21

JAMES 5:17-20

[17] Elijah was a man with a nature like ours, and he prayed fervently that it might not rain, and for three years and six months it did not rain on the earth. [18] Then he prayed again, and heaven gave rain, and the earth bore its fruit. [19] My brothers, if anyone among you wanders from the truth and someone brings him back, [20] let him know that whoever brings back a sinner from his wandering will save his soul from death and will cover a multitude of sins.

Reflecting on God's Word:

1. Elijah is an example of the power of prayer. What prayers did he have answered that were incredible (v. 17-18)? What prayers have you had answered that were also incredible?

_____

_____

_____

_____

_____

2. According to verse 20, returning to God saves your soul from what? How would you respond to someone who thinks the only thing we have to fear is physical death? Is that biblical according to what you read today?

_____

_____

_____

_____

_____

3. According to verse 20, what type of person is being brought back to God? Why do you think James ends his letter with the idea that God is interested in saving sinners?

_____

_____

_____

_____

Application:

Rewrite (either verbatim or in your own words) the verse from today's Scriptures that spoke to you the most. How will you apply today's Scripture in your life?

_____

_____

_____

_____

Praying Through God's Word:

Dear Father God, thank You that You are able to answer our prayers, no matter how big or how small. Lord, I pray that I would not wander from Your truth. Help me to be the kind of person who brings people to You. Thank You for Your goodness and kindness and that You are interested in the lost, the sinful, the imperfect people. Thank You for all that You do for us, God. In Jesus' mighty name I pray. Amen.

CONCLUSION

Congratulations! You have walked your way through the Book of James, and I pray that God has taught you much through His precious Word. Regardless of how slowly or how quickly you made your way through James, rejoice that you have spent time in the Word of God and have read what it has to say to you. Time spent in God's Word is beyond valuable and more precious than we even can begin to realize!

Here are a few final questions...

1. What is something you learned from James that surprised you the most?

_____

_____

_____

_____

_____

2. What is your favorite verse from the entire Book of James?

_____

_____

_____

_____

_____

3. What is the one thing you learned from James that affected you and your walk with the Lord the most?

_____

_____

_____

_____

_____

A final prayer...

Dear Father God, thank You for Your Word and that You are willing to teach people about Yourself and Your ways. Help me to put into action all that I have learned from reading Your Word. Thank You for Your salvation that comes through Jesus alone. It's in His precious name that I pray. Amen.

NOTES

1   Annakeara Stinson, "There's One Big Reason Why You Should Still Write Things Down Whenever You Can," Elite Daily, March 1, 2018, https://www.elitedaily.com/p/does-writing-things-down-help-you-learn-science-says-it-definitely-does-heres-why-8365318.

2   David Guzik, "The Humble Dependence of a True Faith," Blue Letter Bible, July 2021, https://www.blueletterbible.org/Comm/guzik_david/StudyGuide2017-Jam/Jam-4.cfm?a=1150011.

3   David Guzik, "The Humble Dependence of a True Faith," Blue Letter Bible, July 2021, https://www.blueletterbible.org/Comm/guzik_david/StudyGuide2017-Jam/Jam-4.cfm?a=1150011.

ACKNOWLEDGEMENTS

Thank you to my husband, Jonathan, for encouraging me throughout this process. I appreciate your advice and your willingness to listen to me explain all of my ideas (for probably too long of a time).

Thank you to my kiddos, Aubrey, Simon, and Zachary, for (kind of) trying to be quiet while I worked.

Thank you to all of my sweet friends who were willing to listen to me share my vision for this project—in particular, the lovely ladies in my Monday night women's group.

Thank you to Nathan Shireman, Sara Gilham, and Katie Shepard for their valuable feedback and support.

Thank you to my parents for giving me a childhood home where learning was cherished and encouraged.

Above all, thank you to the Lord Jesus Christ for all that He has done for me, including giving me a passion for reading and learning and the opportunity to create something that hopefully helps others while helping me along the way.

Printed in the United States
by Baker & Taylor Publisher Services